Spiritual Life
Prayer Guide
Psalms and Proverbs

Dr. B. Lee Ligon-Borden

Ekklesia Publications
Frisco, Texas

A Spiritual Life Prayer Guide Psalms and Proverbs

ISBN 978-0-9889552-3-3
© 2014 Rev. Dr. B. Lee Ligon-Borden

Published by Ekklesia Publications

Printed in the United States of America

For all book orders:
www.ekk.org

ALL RIGHTS RESERVED

For Information:
Ekklesia Publications • P. O. Box 5343 • Frisco, Texas 75035

This book is dedicated to
my much loved "adopted" Mama,
Betty Robertson,
who has taught the Scriptures
since 1957 to countless believers,
has been a consistent prayer warrior,
has blessed all who know her with her love and infectious laugh,
and has shown us what it means to be
a faithful servant of the Lord Jesus Christ.

Table of Contents

Introduction

The Book of Psalms, used as a hymnal by ancient Israel, covers the entire spectrum of human experience and emotions, from the depths of despair to the height of joy. It provides a pattern for and an example of prayer for each and every occasion in life, from confession through intercession to praise. The third Lubavitcher Rebbe once said that if we only knew the power of Psalms and the effects of its recitation, we would recite them constantly. "Know that the chapters of Psalm shatter all barriers, they ascend higher and still higher with no interference; they prostrate themselves in supplication before the Master of all worlds, and they effect and accomplish with kindness and compassion."[1]

The purpose of this study guide is to set forth a means to use the Psalms and Proverbs in a practical way, as a personal or group study. It has six groupings, each of which has explanations for some of the passages selected, questions to answer, selected Scriptures to memorize, and an opportunity to compose a prayer for group or personal use. If the study is being used in a group, the leader or facilitator might like to expand the explanations into short instructions on the topics prior to using the questions for group sharing and discussion.

No one guide or study is ever complete. Each one is merely an opportunity for spiritual growth for a particular time. Hence, the intent of this guide is merely to provide a "stepping-stone" for your journey of spiritual growth and an introduction into how to use the Psalms for personal prayers.

It is the author's intent and desire that this study will be used for the glory of God, that in "all things He might have the preeminence." (Colossians 1:18b).

Now, to Him who is able to do exceedingly abundantly
above all that we ask or think . . .
(Ephesians 3:20a)

---

[1]   http://www.chabad.org/library/article_cdo/aid/1228223/jewish/Psalms-and-Jewish-Prayer-for-Healing.htm

Week 1
Meditation

This Book of the Law shall not depart from your mouth,
but you shall meditate in it day and night,
that you may observe to do according to all that is written in it.
For then you will make your way prosperous and then you will have good success.
(Joshua 1:8)

We will begin our study with meditation, which provides the basis for what is to follow. There is much misunderstanding about meditation, primarily because of the use of different forms in the New Age movement and by various cults. Meditation, however, is nothing new, and the New Agers do not have a corner on it. In fact, David speaks in numerous Psalms about meditating on God's Word, and other scriptures bear witness to the value of Biblical meditation, as opposed to what other groups offer. So just what is Biblical meditation? Paul gives us some idea in his letter to the Philippians: "Finally, brethren, whatever things are true, whatever things are noble, whatever things are just, whatever things are pure, whatever things are lovely, whatever things are of good report, if there is any virtue and if there is anything praiseworthy – meditate on these things" (Philippians 4:8). Through meditation on God's Word, we gain wisdom and, with it, great blessing:

Happy is the man who finds wisdom,
And the man who gains understanding;
For her proceeds are better than the profits of silver
And her gain than fine gold.
She is more precious than rubies,
And all the things you may desire cannot compare with her.
(Proverbs 3:13-15)

A form that was used by the ancient church since at least the 4th century and that has had a resurgence is called *lectio divina*, meaning "divine reading." In practice, it involves four stages: reading (*lectio*), pondering the text (*meditatio*), praying (*oratio*), and contemplating (*contemplatio*). In Romans 12:2, Paul tells us that we are transformed by the renewing of our minds and that, in doing so, we are able to prove what is the good, acceptable, and perfect will of God. *Lectio divina* is a good way to renew our minds so that we are not conformed to this world. This week's lessons offer a pattern for using this form of meditation.

Day One – Background

In the passages below, what is the focus of the psalmist's meditation:

*Psalm 77:12*_____

_____

*Psalm 119:15*_____

_____

*Psalm 119:27*_____

_____

*Psalm 119:48*_____

_____

*Psalm 119:78*_____

_____

*Psalm 119:97*_____

_____

*Psalm 119:99*_____

_____

Psalm 119:148 _____

_____

*Psalm 145:5*_____

_____

<u>Read Proverbs 1:1-7</u>

How does this passage align with the psalms above?

_____
_____
_____
_____

Memorize

Psalm 119:97
Oh, how I love Your law!
It is my meditation all the day.

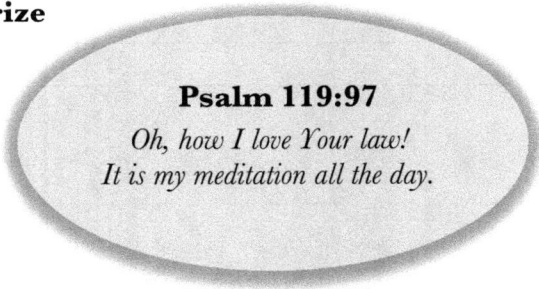

Day Two – Lectio
Reading

<u>Read Psalm 1 *several times*</u>

1. List the 5 characteristics of the righteous person:

_____
_____
_____
_____
_____

2. What metaphor is used to describe the righteous person?

_____

_____

3. What are the results of this way of life?

_____

_____

4. What metaphor is used for the wicked?

_____

_____

5. What is their end?

_____

_____

How does their end differ from that of the righteous?

_____

_____

Memorize

Psalm 1:1-2

Blessed is the man
Who walks not in the counsel of the ungodly,
Nor stands in the path of sinners,
Nor sits in the seat of the scornful;
But his delight is in the law of the Lord,
And in His law he meditates day and night.

Day Three – Meditatio
Meditating

Read Psalm 1 again *several times.*

Pray after each reading, asking God to open new insights.

What word or phrase stands out to you?

_____

_____

Ponder its meaning. Explain what this word or phrase means in *your* life.

_____

_____

_____

_____

_____

_____

_____

_____

Memorize

Psalm 1:3
*He shall be like a tree
Planted by the rivers of water,
That brings forth its fruit in its season,
Whose leaf also shall not whither;
And whatever he does shall prosper.*

Day Four – Oratio
Praying

> *Lord, open my eyes today that I might know the truth of Your Word.*

Where are you today?

Are you one of the blessed, having the righteousness of God accounted on Your behalf through the shed blood of Jesus Christ (Romans 4:5, II Corinthians 5:21)? Or are you still counting on your own righteousness—and counted among "the wicked"? If you have not placed your faith in Jesus Christ for salvation, the Scriptures say that you are still in your condition of sin and you are separated from God (Romans 3:23, 6:23). There is no "magical prayer" for receiving Jesus Christ as your Savior, but these factors are important:

- *admit* your sinful condition before God and your separation from Him (Romans 3:23);
- *recognize* that Jesus Christ, His only Son, shed His blood on the Cross and died for *your* sins, and that He provides the only means of salvation (Matthew 3:17; I Peter 1:18,19; Romans 5:6; John 14:6);
- *repent*, meaning turn *from* your way of life apart from God and *to* God and His provision for you;
- *ask* God to forgive you (I John 1:8, 9);
- *receive* God's gift of salvation, on the basis of His grace alone (Ephesians 2:8-9), and thank Him; and
- *declare* Jesus Christ as your Lord and Savior (Romans 10:9).

If you know the Lord, what characterizes your relationship with Him? Consider how you "meditate." Write a prayer using the Psalms from Day One. Bring it to the class to read if you feel comfortable sharing it.

_____
_____
_____
_____
_____
_____
_____

Memorize

Psalm 1:4
The ungodly are not so,
But are like chaff which the wind drives away.

Day Five – Contemplatio
Contemplating

Re-read Psalm 1 several times.

Then, read one verse at a time and think about what it means in your life.

What word or phrase stands out to you from each verse?

*Verse 1*_____

*Verse 2*_____

*Verse 3*_____

*Verse 4*_____

*Verse 5*_____

*Verse 6*_____

What do you think God is saying to you personally in the Psalm? Write a paragraph in the form of a journal entry stating how this psalm speaks to you in your daily life. Bring it to the class to read if you feel comfortable sharing it.

_____
_____
_____
_____
_____
_____
_____
_____
_____
_____
_____
_____
_____
_____
_____
_____
_____
_____

Memorize

Psalm 1:5-6

Therefore the ungodly shall not stand in the judgment,
Nor sinners in the congregation of the righteous;
For the Lord knows the way of the righteous,
But the way of the ungodly shall perish.

Week 2
Prayer: Laments in Times
of Pain and Suffering

A misconception taught in some faith communities is that Christians should not or will not experience pain and suffering. This unfortunate approach to the Christian life not only is unscriptural but can be extremely defeating and detrimental to the individual who is experiencing illness, grief, loss of job, financial stress, or other adversities of life. Rather than being an evidence of one's lack of faith or of God's indifference or judgment, pain and suffering are part of the maturing process of being conformed to the likeness of Christ (Romans 8:29).

The psalmists knew both pain and suffering, and their prayers to God remind us that we are not alone in our suffering, nor are we alone in times of testing (Hebrews 11:36 – 12:2). The Psalms also provide a way to use God's Word itself to sustain us and to encourage us to trust the One who said He will never leave or forsake us (Matthew 28:20, Hebrews 13:5). These types of Psalms – ones dealing with pain and suffering – are called Laments.

The study this week will look at the psalms that can be particularly helpful in specific times of trial. These selections are by no means exhaustive. They are intended merely to lay a foundation for using the Psalms to seek God's face in times of adversity.

Day One – When Life Doesn't Seem Fair

Have you ever felt that God has forsaken you or that life isn't fair because you are suffering while someone who is clearly not living a godly life seems to do well? Your feelings and questions are not unusual. In fact, Psalm 73 addresses this very issue. Asaph, the writer of this psalm, goes through a process of understanding that God is concerned with long-term consequences and that righteousness eventually prevails – but in God's time, not ours!

<u>Read Psalm 73 several times and then answer the following questions:</u>

Verses 1-3
What was Asaph's dilemma? His sin?

_____

_____

_____

_____

Verses 4-12
How does Asaph describe the "wicked"?

_____

_____

_____

_____

_____

_____

_____

How might this situation apply to *your* life?

_____

_____

_____

_____

_____

_____

_____

_____

Verses 13-16

What reaction does Asaph have as he views the difference between his situation and that of the wicked?

_____

_____

_____

_____

Have *you* ever felt this way? If so, when? What was the outcome?

_____

_____

_____

_____

_____

_____

_____

Verses 17-20

Asaph describes a major change in his perspective. In the study of literature, particularly poetry, this change is referred to as a "major shift" because the entire focus and/or tone changes and the subject moves in a different, even opposite, direction. Asaph's experience is not unusual – we are all susceptible to viewing life from a narrow or biased perspective, one that is of our own making and fails to realize that God has a "bigger picture" and purpose. What "check" in his attitude does he experience? Verse 17 says that the change occurred when he entered the sanctuary of God. This term can mean more than merely a building; "sanctuary" also can mean a place of quiet contemplation. For our purposes, it may mean to enter into an awareness of the presence of God in our lives.

Describe the change in Asaph's perspective:

_____
_____
_____
_____
_____
_____
_____

Verses 21-22
Asaph is honest about his sin. He uses four adjectives (embittered, pierced within, senseless, ignorant) and a simile (like a beast before God) to describe his condition when he viewed life from a temporal, rather than an eternal, perspective. Think of the last time that you were in a similar situation. How would you describe *your* attitude? Have you confessed it to God (I John 1:9)?

_____
_____
_____
_____
_____
_____
_____

Verses 23-24
What confidence in God does Asaph express?

_____
_____

Verses 25-26
As Asaph turns his attention from the temporal to the eternal, from the circumstances to the Creator, he sees life from a different perspective, confesses his sin, and praises and worships God. He expresses his worship in terms of relationship. Use his response as a prayer to God, making it personal, first by emphasizing the first-person pronouns and then by emphasizing the pronouns for God.

_____
_____
_____
_____
_____
_____
_____
_____
_____
_____

Verses 27-28

These verses are a summation of what Asaph has learned. Ultimately, he proclaims that God is his refuge. What have *you* learned about *your* life and relationship with God through this study of Psalm 73?

_____
_____
_____
_____
_____
_____

Read Psalms 37 and 52.

What do these psalms say about the "fairness" of life? How do they compare with Psalm 73? Select one verse from each psalm that is meaningful to you and explain its importance to you.

_____
_____
_____
_____
_____
_____
_____

Memorize

Proverbs 3:5,6
Trust in the Lord with all your heart,
And lean not on your own
understanding; In all your ways
acknowledge Him,
And He shall direct your paths.

Day Two – When Evil Seems to Prevail

Today's lesson builds on yesterday's lesson. Have you experienced intentional attacks against you or your family or someone else? You are not alone. In our day of rampant dishonesty, from the simplest place (try websites for cheating on Words with Friends!) to the actions taken by leaders in different corporations, organizations, and even churches, lies, deceit, maligning—evil—can seem to prevail. The psalmist cries out to God about the distress of seeing the prosperity of those who do evil. We are going to look again at the contrary perspectives of viewing life from a temporal frame of reference, when evil does seem to win out, and from God's eternal perspective, which comforts us by giving us a very different picture.

Read Psalm 64:1-6

The psalmist describes the intentional designs against him by his enemies. Today, plots can still take on sinister forms, and many people have experienced them in their social circles, their places of business, and even, sadly, their places of worship. The psalmist takes his concerns to God, knowing that he can be brutally honest about stating what he is confronting. As you read through these six verses, write down the words the psalmist uses for these categories:

The enemy's strategy (*vss. 2, 5b*)

_____

_____

The enemy's tactics (*vss. 3, 4, 5a*)

_____

_____

The enemy's determination (*vs. 6*)

_____

_____

<u>Read Psalm 56:1-2, 5-7</u>

David wrote this psalm while being pursued and captured by the Philistines. Although it pertains to a precise situation, it is also a description of enemies that are opponents of all that is good and can be extended to the spiritual forces that seek to do us harm (I Peter 5:8). As you read through these verses, write down the words the psalmist uses for these situations:

The extent of the enemy's attack (*vss. 1b, 2a, 5a*). What phrase does the psalmist use consistently

_____

_____

_____

_____

The enemy's strategy (*vss. 2b, 5b, 6b*)

_____

_____

_____

_____

The enemy's tactics (*vss. 2a, 5a, 6a*)

_____
_____
_____
_____

Read Psalm 59:1-3, 6-7, 14-15

Again, the Psalm refers to a specific incident in David's life (when King Saul was attempting to kill him) but has relevance for us today in the spiritual battle in which we are engaged and which manifests in situations in our lives. As you read through these verses, write down the words the psalmist uses for these situations.

How does David describe the enemy? (*vss. 1, 2*)

_____
_____
_____

What actions is the enemy taking?

*Verse 3a*_____
*Verse 3b*_____
*Verse 4a*_____
*Verse 6*_____
*Verse 7*_____
*Verse 14*_____

Viewing life from a temporal frame of reference:

Who *seems* to be "winning"?

_____
_____

To whom does the psalmist appeal? Note specific terms, and the psalmist's expression of trust:

*Psalm 56:1*_____

_____

*Psalm 56:4*_____

_____

*Psalm 56:10*_____

_____

*Psalm 56:11*_____

_____

*Psalm 59:1*_____

*Psalm 59:5*_____

_____

*Psalm 59:8*_____

_____

*Psalm 59:9*_____

_____

*Psalm 59:10*_____

_____

*Psalm 59:11b*_____

_____

*Psalm 59:17b*_____

_____

What is the psalmist's comfort and confidence?

*Psalm 56:9, 13*_____

_____

*Psalm 58:11*_____

_____

*Psalm 64:7-8*_____

_____

How does the eternal perspective differ from the temporal perspective?

_____

_____

_____

Write a short prayer concerning an event in your own life (or the common spiritual warfare of all believers), incorporating the main points of these psalms: the situation, the emotions, the confidence in God, praise of God.

_____

_____

_____

_____

_____

_____

_____

_____

Memorize

Psalm 59:17

*To you, O my Strength, I will sing
praises; For God is my defense
My God of mercy.*

Day Three – When God Seems Far Away

As we grow in our Christian experience, we find that the journey occasionally involves valleys as well as mountaintops. Sometimes those valleys seem very deep and very dark. In fact, one of the great leaders of the Church, Saint John of the Cross, coined the term "dark night of the soul" in a poem about the process of Christian maturity (not to be confused with some of the use of the term in New Age movements). He saw these dark nights as times of purification, first of the senses and, second, of the spirit. During those times, God *seems* very far away. The psalmists expressed the feelings that accompany these times, and their words may serve as a means of encouragement to us in these times, as well as good models for prayers. Keep in mind that our Lord Jesus Christ knows and understands these times better than we can ever imagine, for He went through the darkest night ever experienced when he took upon Himself the sins of the world. It was in that darkest of dark moments that He experienced in our place the eternal separation from the Father that we all deserve and cried, "My God, my God, Why hast Thou forsaken me?" Psalm 22, a psalm of David, is considered one of the many Messianic psalms because it so vividly expresses not only the situation David faced but also the experience of our Lord on the cross. Indeed, it is Psalm 22 that Jesus Christ quoted on the cross. Those words express the emotions that the believer also may experience – that God has forsaken her or him. Another Psalm that deals with the dark night of the soul is Psalm 13, and we will use it today for our study.

Read Psalm 13

Verses 1-2
What refrain (repeated phrase) is found in these verses?

_____

What does this phrase imply about the psalmist's situation?

_____

_____

What specific terms does the psalmist use to express his feelings?

*Verse 1a*_____

*Verse 1b*_____

*Verse 2b*_____

*Verse 2c*_____

When was the last time that *you* felt this way? What was happening in *your life?*

_____

_____

_____

_____

Rephrase this description in the form of a prayer, telling God what you felt (or feel, if are going through a problem right now).

_____

_____

_____

_____

_____

_____

_____

_____

Verse 3a

What appeal does the psalmist make? To whom does he make it?

_____

_____

Upon what does he base his appeal?

*Verse 3b*_____

*Verse 4a*_____

*Verse 4b*_____

A shift occurs in Verses 5-6. The psalmist turns from his anguish to a statement of faith. What does he say about the past and present?

*Verse 5a*_____

What does he say about the future?

*Verse 5b*_____

_____

*Verse 6*_____

_____

Read Psalm 42:9-11

What familiar phrase do you find in this passage? *(vss. 9-10)*

_____

_____

How is the psalmist's response in this psalm similar to that in the previous psalm (13) *(vs. 11)*

_____

_____

As an expression of faith in God's goodness, thank Him in the midst of these situations. Giving thanks brings us back to an awareness of God's love and sovereignty and reminds us that He has promised to work *ALL* things together for good for those who love Him and are called according to His purpose (Romans 8:28). Some people like to declare the short statement: "God is good – ALL the time!" You may also want to claim the promise of Jeremiah 29:11. In your own words, write a prayer or psalm about your experience of darkness, using the terms recorded in these psalms.

_____

_____

_____

_____

_____

_____

Memorize

Psalm 42:11
Why are you cast down, O my soul?
And why are you disquieted within me?
Hope in God;
For I shall again praise Him,
The help of my countenance and my God.

Day Four – When You Suffer Physical Illness or other Distress

Physical illness, especially when it is prolonged, can lead to discouragement and depression, anger and frustration. Although God often heals quickly, other times illness may extend for a long period of time and have numerous ongoing challenges. Everyone's experience of healing is different, but the emotions are similar, and God understands our feelings (Psalm 139:2 KJV). In the readings below, note how the Psalms represent all kinds of feelings we may experience when we suffer, especially when we suffer prolonged physical illness. Write down what the psalmist is experiencing and note if *you* have ever had this feeling and, if so, when. We will look more at praying for healing in next week's lessons.

Read Psalm 22:1-2

Have you ever felt like this? What were your circumstances? To whom or what did you turn?

_____

_____

_____

_____

_____

_____
_____
_____
_____
_____

Read Matthew 28:20 and Hebrews 13:5b

What promise does Jesus make?

_____
_____

Read Psalm 25:16-18, 20

What words does the psalmist use to express emotions (_vs. 16a, 17b_)? Have you ever felt like this? To whom or what did you turn?

_____
_____
_____
_____

What does it mean to you to "take refuge" in the Lord? (_vs. 20b_)

_____
_____
_____
_____
_____

Read Deuteronomy 33:27a

What image does this have for you?

_____
_____

Write out a statement or declaration of what these verses mean to you:

_____

_____

_____

_____

_____

_____

_____

_____

_____

Read Psalm 38:5-11

What are some of the phrases used to describe the psalmist's condition?

_____

_____

_____

_____

Read Psalm 38:15

To whom does the psalmist turn?

_____

Have _you_ ever felt like this? To whom or what did you turn?

_____

_____

What comfort could you offer someone else in this situation?

_____

_____

_____

_____

Read Psalm 88:13-18

Have *you* ever felt like this? To whom or what did you turn?

_____

_____

Read Psalm 89:1-2

How do these words contrast with those in Psalm 88?

_____

_____

_____

_____

_____

_____

Read Psalm 71:20-21

What four expectations doe the psalmist have for the future?

a._____

b._____

c._____

d._____

Using phrases from the above Psalms, or your own words that you
filled in, write out a prayer to God.

_____

_____
_____
_____
_____

Once you have expressed your feelings honestly, <u>read Psalm 25:4-5</u> and then express your faith in God's goodness and praise His holy name. Add below your praise to your prayer:

_____
_____
_____
_____
_____
_____
_____
_____

Memorize

Psalm 25:4-5

Show me Your ways, O Lord;
Teach me your paths.
Lead me in Your truth and teach me,
For you are the God of my salvation;
On You I wait all the day.

Day Five – When a Loved One Dies

We sometimes refer to the death of a Christian as that person's "homecoming" or "coronation day," and certainly deep within most of us is the joy of knowing our loved one is with the Lord and our separation is only temporary. This knowledge, however, does not necessarily ease the pain of grief, which is a valid emotion and requires that we allow God to take us through the grief process and heal us. Many good studies on grief, as well as Christian ministries devoted to dealing with grief, are available. The grieving process takes some time, so today's lesson does not attempt to address all the areas of healing and comfort an individual may need, and the author recommends that one who is grieving seek out someone--a priest, pastor, counselor, or friend--to help with that process. Nonetheless, the Psalms in today's study should be valuable, and they may be useful in helping others deal with grief.

<u>Read Psalm 116:15</u>

What does it say about the death of God's child?

_____

_____

What does that mean to *you* regarding *your* loved one?

_____

_____

Rephrase the scripture putting in the name of your loved one:

_____

_____

Rephrase it giving thanks to God regarding your loved one:

_____

_____

<u>Read Psalm 34:18</u>

What does it say about the Lord in times of grief?
a. _____
b. _____

God desires to comfort you and hold you in this time of grief.

Read Psalm 46:1

Reword it as a declaration of personal faith using first-person (I, me, my):

_____

_____

_____

_____

_____

A good quotation about death comes from William Penn (*Some Fruits of Solitude/More Fruits of Solitude*):

> *"They that love beyond the world cannot be separated by it.*
> *Death cannot kill what never dies."*

Read Psalm 30:5c-d

What does it say about (a) the present and (b) the future? Put these phrases in your own words:

a. _____

_____

b. _____

_____

Read Psalm 71:5,6

Turn it into a personal declaration of praise:

_____

_____

_____

_____

_____

_____

Memorize

Psalm 30:5b

Weeping may endure for a night,
But joy comes in the morning.

Week 3
Prayer: Intercession and Supplication

In Week 2, we looked at laments. We saw how we can use the Psalms as prayers in those difficult times in our lives when we need to cry out to God on our behalf –to reassure us, to guide us, to protect us, to comfort us. This week, we will look at two other types of prayer: intercession, which is prayer for others, and supplication, which is prayer for ourselves in various situations. The Gospels record times when our Lord Jesus Christ offered both types of prayers.

Intercessory prayer involves great commitment and responsibility. The Scriptures record numerous times when the prayers of one person or one nation changed the course of history. For instance, Abraham persisted in prayer when God was going to destroy Sodom (Genesis 18:23-32), and Moses interceded for the people of God, pleading that they not be destroyed (Exodus 32:7-14; Deuteronomy 9:8-9; Psalm 106:23). In Acts 12, we learn that the church prayed without ceasing when Peter was in jail, and his chains fell off and he walked out. In His high priestly prayer, our Lord prayed for you and me (John 17).

We are told that God seeks those who will intercede on behalf of others (II Chronicles 16:9, Ezekiel 22:30). In addition to requiring perseverance, self-discipline, and responsibility, intercessory prayer also may involve fasting. Although some people have a specific calling to be intercessors, all believers are called to intercessory prayer, to pray for one another. Our prayers on behalf of others may take many forms, and often come at the request of the individual or that person's loved ones. We will look at specific Psalms that can be used in different circumstances when praying for others and for ourselves.

Day One – Praying for Family Members

Our first responsibility, after our relationship with God, is our family. The needs of families vary, of course, but there are certain prayers that we can pray – for them to seek God, to be safe, to make wise decisions, to be protected. Some of Paul's prayers in his epistles can be used very effectively, and so can the Psalms. One of the most important responsibilities we have is to teach our children, even as God instructed the Israelites to teach their children.

For today's study, we are going to use Psalms 67 and 91, based on God's direction to Moses in the Wilderness regarding blessing our families *(Numbers 6:22-26)*:

> *And the LORD spoke to Moses, saying: "Speak to Aaron and his sons, saying,*
> *'This is the way you shall bless the children of*
> *Israel. Say to them: "The LORD bless you*
> *and keep you;*
> *The LORD make His*
> *face shine upon you,*
> *And be gracious to you;*
> *The LORD lift up His countenance upon you,*
> *And give you peace."'*

Read Psalm 67

Verse 1
What three things does the Psalmist request that God do?
a. _____
b. _____
c. _____
For your family, what would it mean (in specific, practical, actual terms) to you for God to

a. "be gracious"

_____

_____

b. "bless you"

_____

_____

c. "make His face shine upon you"

_____

_____

Verse 2

Note that the psalmist has a greater purpose in mind than merely having a blessing upon his own life and his family. What outcome does the psalmist want from this blessing?

_____

Read Psalm 91

This Psalm is often used as a prayer for protection. It is also a statement of faith concerning God's steadfast love.

Verse 1

What confidence does the psalmist express in God's protection?

_____

_____

Verse 2

What terms does the psalmist use for God? What difference do you see in these terms?

a. _____

_____

b. _____

_____

Although much of the Psalm uses the second-person singular pronoun, it can be converted into a prayer in the first- or third-person. Using verses 3-16, rewrite the passages either as a prayer, making it personal by inserting first-person pronouns (I, me, my) or the name of a specific family member(s).

Examples using verse 3:
Prayer: Deliver_____(name the individual) from the snare of the fowler and from the deadly pestilence.
Declaration: God will deliver_____from the snare of the fowler and from the deadly pestilence.

Your prayer/declaration:

_____

_____

_____

_____

_____

_____

_____

_____

_____

_____

Memorize

II Chronicles 16:9

For the eyes of the Lord run to and fro throughout the whole earth, to show Himself strong on behalf of those whose heart is loyal to Him.

Day Two – Praying for the Lost

Today, we are going to approach the Psalms from a different direction and use one of the Psalms that relates God's goodness to His people to pray for those who do not know Him. Our study will come from a portion of Psalm 107, looking at four different conditions of humanity as examples of those who are lost. We then will take the psalmist's descriptions of God's saving grace for those who have come to Him from various walks of life and pray for people who are lost or in dire circumstances.

Read Psalm 107:1-32

Verse 1
The Psalm begins with thanksgiving and praise of God, as should all our prayers. What, specifically, is the source of thanksgiving?

_____

_____

Verse 2
To whom is the exhortation for thanksgiving given? How are they described?

_____

_____

_____

Verse 3
What is the extent of the origin of this Body of people?

_____

_____

Group 1 *Verses 4-7*
How is this group described? *(vss. 4, 5)*

_____

_____

_____

_____

What group of people (or individual) in your life or experience might be described in these terms?

_____

_____

_____

_____

What did they do? *(vs. 6)*

_____

_____

What was God's response? *(vss. 6b, 7)*

_____

_____

Group 2 *Verses 10-14*

How is this group described? *(vs. 10)*

_____

What caused them to be in this condition *(vs. 11)*

_____

What consequences did they experience? *(vs. 12)*

_____

What did they do? *(vs. 13)*

_____

What was God's response? *(vs. 14)*

_____

Group 3 *Verses 17-20*

How is this group described? (*vs. 17a*)

_____

What did they do? (*vs. 17a*)

_____

What consequences did they experience? (*vss. 17b, 18*)

_____

_____

What group of people (or individual) in your life or experience might be described in these terms?

_____

_____

What did they do? (*vs. 19*)

_____

_____

What was God's response? (*vss. 19b, 20*)

_____

_____

Group 4 *Verses 23-29*

How is this group described? (*vs. 23*)

_____

What did they experience? (*vss. 24, 25*)

_____

How might this description be applied metaphorically to everyday circumstances?

_____

_____

_____

Have you ever felt like you were in the midst of a great storm of life? If so, when?

_____

_____

What was their response to adversity? (*vss. 26, 27*)

_____

_____

What did they do? (*vs. 28*)

_____

_____

What was God's response? (*vs. 29-30*)

_____

_____

What *pattern* do you see in *all* of these groups?

_____

_____

_____

_____

Read Verses 8, 15, 21, 31
The repetition serves as a refrain of praise. Write out the words here:

_____

_____

_____

Verses 9, 16
How is God described?

_____

_____

_____

Verses 22
What response are they called upon to offer?

_____

_____

Read Verses 33-43

Verses 33-38
Summarize the psalmist's descriptions of God's benevolences.

_____

_____

_____

_____

Verses 39-42
What contrast is depicted?

_____

_____

_____

Verse 43
What is the response of the wise person to what has been described above?

_____

_____

48

_____

_____

Construct a prayer for someone you know who fits one of the descriptions above, using the description and God's response.

Example:

Lord, I praise You that You_____. I pray for_____, who is like the ones described in Group_____.   Your word shows that you_____. I ask that you would_____. Thank you that (vs. 10)_____. Etc.

_____

_____

_____

_____

_____

_____

_____

_____

_____

_____

Memorize

Psalm 107:1,2

Oh give thanks to the Lord, for He is good,
For his mercy endures forever.
Let the redeemed of the Lord say so,
Whom He has redeemed from the hand of the enemy.

Day Three – Praying for our Nation and Leaders

In our day of partisan rivalry here in the U.S. and elsewhere, it is important to remember that God has called upon His people to pray for the leaders of their country, whether or not they are in agreement with their leadership. Indeed, God has placed the responsibility for having a righteous, healed nation upon *His* people. In II Chronicles 7:14, He says, "if MY people, who are called by MY name, will humble themselves and pray and seek my face and turn from their wicked ways, then will I hear from heaven and heal their land." (emphasis is mine). Also, Paul in writing to Timothy, urged that "supplications, prayers, intercessions, and thanksgiving be made for all people, for kings and all who are in high positions, that we may lead a peaceful and quiet life" (I Timothy 2:1). Psalm 72:1-16 provides a good model for praying for the leader of one's country or the leaders of other countries of the world. Today, we will explore a portion of Psalm 72 as a basis for praying for our President and other leaders in our government.

Read Psalm 72:1-11

Although Psalm 72 is a Royal Psalm that speaks of David's line and looks forward to the worldwide rule of the Messiah, it has certain elements that can rightly be prayed for any leader. We are going to look at how these requests can be used today for our own leaders.

Verse 1

What two attributes does the psalmist ask God to give the leader?

a. _____

b. _____

Turn this request into a prayer for our President and other leaders:

_____

_____

_____

Verse 2

What does the psalmist request regarding the king's leadership?

a. _____

b. _____

Turn this request into a prayer for our President and other leaders:

_____

_____

_____

_____

Verse 3

What does the psalmist request for the economy?

_____

_____

Turn this request into a prayer for our country:

_____

_____

_____

_____

Verse 4

What does the psalmist request regarding the king's leadership?

a. _____

b. _____

c. _____

Turn this request into a prayer for our President and other leaders:

_____

_____

_____

_____

Verse 5

The psalmist asks that "they" might fear the Lord. How would you state this request in a prayer for all of our leaders?

_____

_____

_____

_____

_____

Verse 6

This request uses two similes. What two images are drawn?

a._____

_____

b._____

_____

What do *you* think these similes represent?

_____

_____

_____

How would you word this thought in a prayer for our President? When you have completed writing the prayer, pray it in earnest.

_____

_____

_____

_____

_____

_____

_____

_____

Verse 7

What does the psalmist request concerning social aspects?

_____

_____

_____

Verses 8-11

These verses address the superiority with regard to the different nations of the world. Read this passage several times and then write a prayer for our nation in relation to the other nations of the world, using some of these images or descriptions.

_____

_____

_____

_____

_____

_____

Verses 12-14

These verses speak of the leader as caring for others. How might these verses be reworded in the context of praying for our needs within our own nation?

*Verse 12*_____

_____

*Verse 13*_____

_____

*Verse 14*_____

_____

Verse 16

This verse is a powerful appeal for blessing upon the land. Reword this prayer using it specifically for your nation.

_____

_____

_____

_____

_____

_____

_____

_____

Memorize

II Chronicles 7:14

*If My people, who are called by My name
will humble themselves, and pray
and seek My face,
and turn from their wicked ways,
then I will hear from heaven,
and will forgive their sin, and heal their land.*

Day Four – Praying for Healing

There are many ways to use the Psalms and Proverbs to pray for ourselves when we are afflicted and for others who are ill. Our Jewish friends have a custom in praying for the ill, which is to recite the following Psalms: 6, 9, 13, 16, 17, 18, 20, 22, 23, 28, 30, 31, 32, 33, 37, 38, 39, 41, 49, 55, 56, 69, 86, 88, 89, 90, 91, 102, 103, 104, 107, 116, 118, 142, 143, and 148. Afterwards, they recite the stanzas from Psalm 119 that correspond to the letters of the ill individual's Jewish name(s). Psalm 119 is an acrostic with 22 stanzas; each stanza has eight verses, each of which begins with the same letter from the Hebrew alphabet, in alphabetical order. For instance, the eight verses of the first stanza all begin with the letter *aleph;* the next stanza is composed of eight verses all beginning with *bet;* in the third stanza, all the eight verses begin with *gimel,* and so forth. As an example, if the person's name is Moshe (משה), one would recite the stanzas that begin with *mem, shin,* and *hey.* For example, if the person's name is Rachel (רלח), the stanzas that begin with *resh, chet* and *lamed* would be recited.

Other schemes also can be used. One is to call upon God by one of His many names that refer to our relationship with Him, as our Lord, Shield, Shepherd, Deliverer, Provider, and so forth, and then to proceed with petition or request, praise, thanksgiving, and confidence in the future. We will use this latter approach in our study today.

a. Call upon the name of the Lord and His work on your behalf. Look up the following verses and write down what they mean to you with regard to God and His dealings with *you* and others, putting them in your *own* words:

*Psalm 18.1-2*_____

_____

_____

*Psalm 23:1*_____

_____

_____

*Psalm 88:1-2*_____

_____

_____

*Psalm 121:1-2*_____

_____

_____

*Psalm 141:5*_____

_____

_____

b. The psalmists often <u>cried to God to hear them</u>. Look up the following verses and write down the psalmists' words:

*Psalm 7:1*_____

_____

_____

*Psalm 55:1*_____

_____

_____

*Psalm 61:1*_____

_____

_____

*Psalm 64:1*_____

_____

_____

c. Next <u>praise the Lord</u> concerning His care for you and/or the person for whom you are praying:

*Psalm 23:2-3*_____

_____

_____

*Psalm 23:4*_____

_____

_____

*Psalm 37:39-40*_____

_____

_____

d. Express your thanksgiving for God's faithfulness and goodness toward you and others:

*Psalm 18:6*_____

_____

_____

*Psalm 22:3-5*_____

_____

_____

*Psalm 22:26*_____

_____

_____

e. Proclaim your confidence in the future and in God's goodness:

*Psalm 23:6*_____

_____

_____

*Psalm 42:5, 11*_____

_____

_____

*Psalm 65:1-4*_____

_____

_____

Memorize

Proverbs 30:5
Every word of is pure;
He is a shield to those who put their trust in Him.

Day Five – Praying for Protection from Evil

Most of us have encountered people who seem to have some evil intent toward us. Some of us have had difficult dealings with neighbors, bosses, family members, or even people in the church who have sought to do us harm. We also live in a precarious age and society, in which unexpected circumstances may put us in dangerous environments. Paul tells us that behind these people's actions and other dire circumstances is an archenemy who seeks to steal, kill, and destroy (I Peter 5:8; John 10:10). Many people are unaware of the many evil influences in our society, but we can rest assured that our heavenly Father is protecting us and calling us to pray for protection in specific circumstances. We can have confidence in God's protection. In Week Two, Day Two, we addressed those times when evil seems to prevail for extended periods of time. Today, we are looking at psalms to use as prayers for protection against evil in specific situations. One of the best known verses from the Psalms concerning God's protection is Psalm 23:4:

Yea, though I walk through the valley of the shadow of death,
I will fear no evil, for You are with me;
Your rod and Your staff, they comfort me.

Memorize this verse if you have not done so already.

Psalms 31, 32, 70, 71, and 91 are powerful prayers for protection from evil and from those who would do harm to us. Select specific verses that speak to you concerning protection from evil and write them down.

_____
_____
_____
_____
_____
_____
_____
_____
_____

What impresses you particularly about the following passages?

Psalm 31:1-3

_____
_____
_____

Psalm 31:4-24

_____
_____
_____

Psalm 70

_____
_____
_____

Psalm 71:1-6

_____

_____

_____

_____

Psalm 71:7-16

_____

_____

_____

_____

Psalm 71:17-24

_____

_____

_____

_____

Using any or all of the Psalms above, or the phrases you wrote down, write out a prayer asking God to protect you and affirming your faith in His steadfast love and care for you.

_____

_____

_____

_____

_____

_____

_____

_____

_____

_____

_____

Memorize

Psalm 6:8-10:
Depart from me, all you workers of iniquity;
For the Lord has heard the voice of my weeping.
The Lord has heard my supplication;
The Lord receives my prayer.
Let all my enemies be ashamed and greatly troubled;
Let them turn back and be ashamed suddenly.

Week 4
Confession, Repentance, and Forgiveness

A word that we don't hear much these days, even in many churches, is *sin* It's a word that has become increasingly unpopular because people don't want to subject themselves to the authority of God in their lives. Instead, they want to, as the words of the Frank Sinatra song go, "do it my way!" Our culture is particularly characterized by the "pull-yourself-up-by-your-bootstraps" mentality and actually encourages and honors the "individuality" that is associated with doing things one's own way. The rejection of God's authority is, of course, nothing new (indeed, it is the very sin of Lucifer; Isaiah 14:12-14). The Psalmist tells us that we all have sinned and "there is none who does good, not even one" (Psalm 53:3).

King David of old was keenly aware of the consequences of following the desires of one's own heart and turning from God's Word and His law. His plummet into the depths of sin and degradation began with a seemingly simple problem: irresponsibility. He failed to lead his troops into war, the responsibility of a good leader, and stayed home to languish instead. A simple matter? Not really, for he rejected his God-given responsibilities. His moral decline was a progression from irresponsibility to laziness to lust to adultery to manipulation and deception to murder (II Samuel 11,12). When he was finally forced to face the extent of his sin, he cried out to God. His prayer is recorded in Psalm 51. It provides a good pattern and way for us to confess our sins, as well.

Day One – Prayer of Confession

Read Psalm 51 several times.

After you have read it through, consider carefully one verse at a time.

Verse 1
To what does David appeal in his cry to God?

_____

_____

Verse 2
What does David ask God to do?

_____

_____

Verse 3
What does David acknowledge before God?

_____

_____

Verse 4
Although David had committed adultery, manipulation, betrayal, and murder that involved other people, what does he say about his (and our) sin?

_____

_____

Why do you think he says, "against *thee only* have I sinned"?

_____

_____

_____

_____

_____

Verses 5-6
What hope or expectation does David have?

_____

_____

Verses 7-12
David's cry to God is worded in different ways. Write out the different requests David makes of the Lord regarding his sin:

*Verse 7a*_____

*Verse 7b*_____

*Verse 8a*_____

*Verse 9a*_____

*Verse 9b*_____

*Verse 10a*_____

*Verse 10b*_____

*Verse 11a*_____

*Verse 11b*_____

*Verse 12a*_____

*Verse 12b*_____

Select several of these phrases and explain what the mean in *your* life.

_____

_____

_____

_____

_____

_____

_____

Write a short prayer that includes some of these verses.

_____

_____

_____

_____

_____

_____

_____

_____

Verses 14-17

In the middle of verse 14, a "shift" occurs in the text. The focus moves from asking God for forgiveness to a song of praise and worship. David expresses his awareness that God is the *God of his salvation*. He realizes that God is not interested in external forms of worship. What does David say is the sacrifice that God honors?

_____

_____

_____

_____

_____

_____

Read Psalm 53

Memorize

Psalm 53:2-3

God looks down from heaven upon the children of men,
To see if there are any who understand, who seek God.
Every one of them has turn aside;
They have together become corrupt;
There is none who does good, No, not one.

Day Two – Wisdom of Confession

Proverbs has much to say about living a righteous life. It also speaks to the danger of living a life of sin. It addresses the kind of life that David chose for a while. Today, the focus is on the destruction that can come from living a life characterized by sin and failing to confess our sins to God. What do the following Scriptures say about the wicked (unbelievers; those who continue to sin without confessing it):

*Proverbs 1:15-19*_____

_____

*Proverbs 4:19*_____

_____

*Proverbs 6:12-14*_____

_____

*Proverbs 10:6b*_____

_____

*Proverbs 11:20a*_____

_____

*Proverbs 13:5b*_____

_____

Do any of these terms describe *your* behavior? If so, which ones?

_____

_____

What was their outcome?

*Proverbs 6:15*_____

_____

*Proverbs 10:16b*_____

_____

*Proverbs 11:5b*_____

_____

*Proverbs 24:16b*_____

_____

Using these Proverbs, write a summation describing the wicked and the consequences of their behaviors/condition:

_____
_____
_____
_____
_____
_____
_____
_____
_____
_____
_____

Memorize

Psalm 51:17
The sacrifices of God are a broken spirit,
A broken and a contrite heart —
These, O God, You will not despise.

Day Three – Prayer of Repentance

God calls us to repentance. Repentance is an interesting word. Many people think that repentance means merely acknowledging one's sin before God and then going about the same old way of life, confessing the same sin again, committing it again, and so forth. On the other hand, some people have the notion that repentance means berating oneself over and over about a sin that has been confessed—and forgiven. Neither concept is accurate. The word *repentance* involves a volitional, deliberate change of mind and behavior, a choice to turn *from* something and *toward* something else. So, when we truly repent of our sins, we confess them and then we turn *from* that manner of life and *to* God's ways. The Psalms are full of examples of turning *from* one's old ways and *to* a new way of life characterized by seeking and serving God. Today, we are going to look at another Psalm by David, Psalm 32, as an example of repentance. For further insights, you might want to look at Psalm 86.

<u>Read Psalm 32</u>

Verses 1-2
This Psalm begins with a song of praise concerning one who has been forgiven. David names four ways in which an individual is blessed after confessing sin:

a._____

b._____

c._____

d._____

Verses 3-4
How does David describe his experience before he confessed his sin to God?

a._____

b._____

c._____

d._____

What do these verses say to you about the consequences of sin?

_____

_____

_____

_____

_____

_____

Verses 5-6

What does David finally do – what words does he use to describe this action? What is the result? What does he say generally about confession of sin?

_____

_____

_____

_____

Verse 7

David has turned from his sin; now he has a completely different experience – instead of hiding from God, he describes his confidence in his newly restored relationship. It is a song of faith. What stands out to you in this verse?

_____

_____

_____

Verses 8-9

This portion of the Psalm has a different "speaker." Some scholars say it may be David taking a different position now that he is healed and has learned from his experience, but more likely the speaker is the Lord.

In the former reading, David expresses his concept of God's role in his life. What is particularly meaningful go you?

_____

_____

_____

_____

_____

Verse 10
These verses contrast the wicked and the one who trusts in God. What can the wicked expect?

_____

What will the one who trusts in the Lord experience?

_____

Verse 11
What does God call each of us who has repented to do?

_____

_____

As you contemplate David's experience – his sin, confession, and repentance, ask God to reveal to you what you need to acknowledge to Him:

_____

_____

How would David's experience of repentance relate to you? Remember that sin is not limited to wicked actions; it is anything that deprives us of experiencing God's best, and it can even include pride in our "good" works! What have you forsaken or turned *from*, and what have you embraced or turned *to*? Be specific. You may want to share this with your study group, but this is primarily a time for you to be honest with yourself.

_____

_____

_____

_____

_____

_____

Memorize

Psalm 32:1,2
Blessed is he whose transgression is forgiven,
Whose sin is covered,
Blessed is the man to whom the Lord does not impute iniquity,
And in whose spirit there is no deceit.

Day Four – Wisdom of Repentance

On Day Two, we saw that the Proverbs have much to say about living a righteous life and the consequences of living a life of sin. It addresses the kind of life that David chose for a while. We looked at the destruction that can come from failing to confess our sins to God. Today, the focus is on the righteous one (who has confessed his/her sin and is in fellowship with God; I John 1:9). Look up the following verses and fill in what they have to say about the righteous.

Proverbs 2:7-8 _____

Proverbs 4:18 _____

Proverbs 9:6a _____

Proverbs 10:16a _____

Proverbs 11:8a _____

Proverbs 11:20b _____

Proverbs 13:21b _____

Proverbs 14:32b _____

*Proverbs 15:9b*_____
*Proverbs 20:7*_____
*Proverbs 22:4*_____
*Proverbs 24:16a*_____
*Proverbs 28:5b*_____
*Proverbs 28:20a*_____
*Proverbs 30:5b*_____

Using these Proverbs, write a summation paragraph about the righteous.

_____
_____
_____
_____
_____
_____
_____
_____
_____

Identify the areas of your life that need to be confessed. Ask the Holy Spirit to search your heart and reveal what needs to be brought before God and what you need to do to repent – to turn *from* this sin and *to* a different way of life that honors God. This is *not* a matter of "works salvation" or trying to "pull yourself up by the bootstraps." It *is* a matter of committing and submitting your life to God and walking in a manner that is pleasing to Him, through the empowerment of the Holy Spirit. You may want to write down what the Holy Spirit reveals to you:

_____
_____
_____
_____
_____
_____
_____

The well-known hymn by Frances R. Havergal, based on Romans 12:1, is a good reminder for this type of understanding of being committed to the Lord. The first verse goes like this:

Take my life and let it be
Consecrated, Lord, to Thee.
Take my moments and my days,
Let them flow in endless praise.

Memorize

Romans 12:1,2

I beseech you therefore, brethren, by the mercies of God,
that you present your bodies a living sacrifice, holy, acceptable to God,
which is your reasonable service.
And do not be conformed to this world,
but be transformed by the renewing of your mind, that you may prove
what is that good and acceptable and perfect will of God.

Day Five – God's Forgiveness

We learn from I John 1:9 that God is *faithful* and *just* to forgive us our sins and to cleanse us of *all* unrighteousness, even the unrighteousness that we don't even know we have! The psalmists put this truth into songs of praise. God's forgiveness is on the basis of the shed blood of the Lord Jesus Christ, for without the shedding of blood, there is no remission for sin (Hebrews 9:22). Today, we are going to look at various verses and make them very personal. Using the following verses, write down first what the psalmist says and then a second time make it personal with an affirmation of thanksgiving.

An example is this:

<u>Psalm 85:2</u>

a.   You have forgiven the iniquity of Your people;/You have covered all their sin.
b.   Thank you, Lord, that you have forgiven my iniquity and covered it in the blood of Christ.

Psalm 32:1
a._____
b._____

Psalm 32:2
a._____
b._____

Psalm 51:7
a._____
b._____

Psalm 86:5
a._____
b._____

Psalm 130:4, 7-8
a._____
b._____

<u>Read I John 1:9 (in the New Testament)</u>

If we confess our sins, what does God promise to do?
a._____
b._____

Combining all the reflections you wrote down for the first parts of the answers above on the Psalms, write out a statement of what God has done on your behalf through the merits of Jesus Christ:

_____

_____

_____

_____

_____

_____

Now, combine all the personal reflections from the second portions of the answers above and compose a <u>prayer of thanksgiving</u> for what God has done for you:

_____

_____

_____

_____

_____

_____

_____

_____

_____

_____

Memorize

I John 1:9
If we confess our sins,
He is faithful and just to forgive us our sins
and to cleanse us from all unrighteousness

Week 5
Praise: Declarative and Descriptive

We hear a lot today about praise – praise services, praising someone at work, praising our children. The word has become so overworked – much like the word *love* – that it often loses its significance with regard to the meaning of praising God. Even some so-called "worship" services do little more than hype the atmosphere and put people into an emotional high or even frenzy. When the Bible speaks of praise, it has a far greater meaning: it focuses on the One being praised, not on how to evoke emotional responses from the person involved. It may include the emotions, but they are not the emphasis.

In the Biblical sense, praise means to extol, laud, and exalt. *Extol* carries with it the sense of glorifying God – giving Him the glory that is rightfully His. In heaven, the angels call out constantly, "Holy, Holy, Holy is the Lord God Almighty" (Revelation 4:8). *To laud* connotes respect or to hold up with honor. *Exalt* means to voice esteem and admiration.

Praise is an important aspect of our relationship with the Lord, partly because we are told to praise Him, so failure to do so is disobedience, but also because it changes our perspective from ourselves and surroundings to the One who created and loves us. Praise is particularly important during those times when it is most difficult to praise—when we are in difficult straits. It strengthens our faith in crises and brings us peace, joy, and confidence.

This week, we will start by looking at Proverbs and what they have to say about praising God. Then, we will look at two different forms of praise Psalms: declarative and descriptive.

Day One – Overview and Proverbs

Proverbs has much to say about appreciating God and praising Him. A term used frequently in Proverbs is "to fear" the Lord. The word "fear" does not mean to be "afraid of," for perfect Love casts out fear. Rather, it means *to hold in esteem, to respect, to hold up with honor.* Because it relates to wisdom, some of the Proverbs we will look at today speak to the value of gaining wisdom, which in turn leads to praise. Contrariwise, there is danger in rejecting wisdom and failing to honor God, which can have grave consequences. Read the Proverbs below and note the main thought or teaching about holding God in high esteem, an aspect of wisdom:

*Proverbs 1:7*_____

_____

*Proverbs 3:34-35*_____

_____

*Proverbs 8:13*_____

_____

*Proverbs 8:17*_____

_____

*Proverbs 9:10-12*_____

_____

*Proverbs 11:20*_____

_____

*Proverbs 14:26*_____

_____

*Proverbs 14:27*_____

_____

*Proverbs 15:16*_____

_____

*Proverbs 18:10*_____

_____

*Proverbs 19:23*_____

_____

Using the Proverbs above, write a summary of what you have learned and how you can incorporate these lessons into your own life.

_____
_____
_____
_____
_____
_____
_____
_____
_____

Now, using what you have learned, turn these truths into a prayer of *praise* to God. You may want to share this prayer with your study group.

_____
_____
_____
_____
_____
_____
_____
_____
_____

Memorize

Proverbs 9:10

The fear of the Lord is the beginning of wisdom,
And knowledge of the Holy One is understanding.

Day Two – Declarative Psalms, Individual

He who offers a sacrifice of thanksgiving
(todah) honors me: and to him who orders his
way aright I shall show the salvation of God.
(Psalm 50:23)

A Psalm of Declarative Praise is sometimes called a Thanksgiving Psalm or *Todah* Psalm. A *todah* psalm gives thanks and praise to God for what He has done (His mighty deeds); it acknowledges His handiwork. There are two types of Declarative Psalms: individual and corporate or group. The first is the praise offered by one person, whereas the latter is the praise given by a community or congregation. Declarative Psalms include 18, 21, 30, 32, 34, 40, 41, 66, 106, 116, and 138. They follow a certain outline:

a. A proclamation of praise or intent to praise ("I will praise…")
b. A summary, retelling of what God has done in the past, report of deliverance or help: ("I cried…He heard…")
c. A renewed vow to praise God
d. Praise of God's mighty acts, a descriptive praise, or a form of instruction based on lessons gained from the experience.

Read Psalm 34

This psalm follows the structure of the Declarative Psalm, praising God and giving instruction, as well as recounting how the Lord has delivered in the past. Much like many of the Proverbs, the instructional portion sets up a contrast between the righteous and the evil or wicked individuals.

After you have read Psalm 34 several times, answer the following questions:

a. Proclamation: *Verses 1-3*

What verbs of praise does David use in these verses?

_____

_____

_____

b. Summary: *Verses 4-7*
This passage describes what God has done for different people. Note what God has done on David's behalf (*vs. 4*), on behalf of other people (*vs. 5*), and on behalf of the needy (*vs. 6*).

David:

_____

The people:

_____

The needy:

_____

Think of a time when God delivered *you* from some type of trouble or answered your need. How would you describe it?

_____

_____

_____

_____

c. Renewed Vows: *Verses 8-10*
The psalmist incorporates into his own praise a call for others to praise God as well. In doing so, he mentions different things for which one should praise God. List them below:

*Verse 8*_____

*Verse 9*_____

*Verse 10*_____

d. Instruction: *Verses 11-22*

In this particular Psalm, the vow is followed by specific instructions; in fact, David calls the children to come and listen to him, and he will teach the fear of the Lord (vs. 11). He mentions both 1) things to avoid or refrain from doing and 2) things to do. What does he say to avoid?

*Verse 13*_____

*Verse 14*_____

In the next three verses, a contrast between the righteous and the wicked or evil is made. What does he say about the righteous?

*Verse 15*_____
_____

*Verse 17*_____
_____

*Verse 18*_____
_____

*Verse 19*_____
_____

*Verse 20*_____
_____

*Verse 22*_____
_____

About the wicked/evil?

*Verse 16*_____

_____

Verse 21

_____

_____

Memorize

Psalm 34:8-9
Oh, taste and see that the Lord is good;
Blessed is the man who trusts in Him!
Oh, fear the LORD, you His saints!
There is no want to those who fear Him.

Day Three – Declarative Psalms, Corporate or Community

The psalms of Declarative Praise also take on a corporate form when the community praises God. They include Psalms 18, 30, 32, 34, 40, 65-67, 75, 90, 92, 95, 103, 106, 124. Somewhat like the personal Declarative Praise psalms, the corporate ones follow a typical structure:

    a. exhortation or call to praise God
    b. a recounting of what God has done in the past
    c. a renewed call to praise

Some of them also have a report of God's intervention.

<u>Read Psalm 104 several times.</u>

It is a "creation psalm," or one that recasts the Genesis record of God's creation of the heavens and the earth. An important note is that the poets of the Old Testament praised God *for* the creation of all nature but, unlike their pagan neighbors, did not deify nature. In other words, they worshipped the God of creation, not the creation itself.

a. Exhortation: *Verses 1-2*
The Psalmist first extols the Lord. What terms are used to describe God?

*Verse 1*_____

*Verse 2*_____

Next, the worshippers recount numerous things God has done. Identify them, summarizing them according to major themes:

Verses 3-4

_____

_____

_____

_____

Verses 5-9

_____

_____

_____

_____

Verses 10-13

_____

_____

_____

_____

Verses 14-18

_____

_____

_____

_____

What does this passage say to you about God's care for all created beings?

_____

_____

_____

What difference does/should this make in our society?

_____

_____

Verses 19-23

_____

_____

_____

_____

What feature or characteristic do all of these verses describe with regard to God?

_____

What difference do these facts make in *your* life?

_____

_____

_____

_____

_____

b. Recounting: *Verses 24-35a*

Verses 24-26
The psalmist summarizes the particular events that have been described in detail previously. What phrase does the psalmist use to summarize all creation?

_____

_____

What two portions of our world does the psalmist praise in this portion?

_____

What is common to both of them?

_____

Verses 27-30
What does this portion of the Psalm say to *you* about God's provision? Make this personal, and write a sentence declaring your confidence in God's provision for *you*:

_____

_____

_____

_____

Verses 31-35a
A shift in focus occurs in verse 31. The poem turns to extol the goodness of God. What do these verses say about God?

_____

_____

_____

_____

Another shift occurs in *verses 33-34*. What distinguishes these two verses from the previous ones?

_____

_____

Put this response in your own words, making this statement personal for *you*.

_____

_____

_____

_____

_____

Verse 35a seems out of place here, at least to many people. How is it different from the other verses?

_____

Why do you think the psalmist made this statement?

_____

_____

_____

c. Renewed calls to praise: *Verse 35b*
In the final verse, the psalmist once again calls for praise.
What terms are used for praise?

_____

_____

_____

Memorize

Psalm 104:33-34

I will sing to the LORD as long as I live;
I will sing praise to my God while I have my being.
May my meditation be sweet to Him;
I will be glad in the LORD.

Day Four – Descriptive Praise, Individual

Psalms of descriptive praise are very similar to those of declarative praise and often the distinction is not made, although they have some discernible differences. Descriptive praise psalms involve a confession or acknowledgment of God's greatness or goodness and an imperative call to praise God. These psalms extoll God's goodness in general by describing His character or attributes. They usually do not address situations of the past but rather focus on God's greatness and His beneficence toward His people and the whole earth (e.g., 29, 33, 34, 47,105, 111, 113, 117, 135, 136, 146, 147). They often are grouped according to sub-genres of Creation Psalms (e.g., 29, 33, 36, 105, 111, 135, 136); Enthronement Psalms, which focus on the Lord's future coming and/or rule (e.g., 47, 93, 95-99); and *Hallel* Psalms (see below). The typical descriptive psalm has this structure:

>   a. *Prologue*, which has some expression of praise (e.g., hallelujah)
>   b. *Cause* for praise, which addresses the character of God (e.g., His greatness, His grace)
>   c. *Exhortation* or renewed call to praise, or a lesson
>   d. *Epilogue*, which is a repeated expression, such as hallelujah, that may (or may not) occur

Read Psalm 33

This psalm follows the four-point structure of a prologue, a call, a cause, and exhortation as epilogue. The psalmist praises YHWH for His faithfulness to protect and deliver.

a. Prologue: *Verses 1-3*
What verbs does the psalmist use in these verses?

*Verse 1*_____

*Verse 2*_____

*Verse 2*_____

*Verse 3*_____

*Verse 3*_____

b. Cause for Praise: *Verses 4-19*

Verses 4-5 describe the Person of YHWH. Summarize these verses noting the many characteristics the psalmist provides:

_____
_____
_____
_____
_____
_____

Verses 6-9 address creation. In verses 6-8, we have a description of God's power in creation, and in verse 9, that description is summarized. What does verse 9 mean to *you*?

_____
_____
_____
_____
_____
_____

Verses 10-12 speak of God's actions with regard to the nations, showing His power and greatness. What does the psalmist say with regard to the nation that honors the Lord?

_____
_____

Verses 13-15 expand upon God's grace and knowledge of the individual. From these verses, what stands out to *you* regarding God's dealings with the individual?

_____
_____
_____

Verses 16-17 emphasize the power of God in all circumstances. What is implied in these verses?

_____

_____

_____

Verses 18-19 focus on the individual who fears the Lord. Summarize these verses:

_____

_____

_____

_____

_____

c. Exhortation: *Verses 20-21*

Although the psalmist's words describe the attitude of the righteous, they also form an exhortation or encouragement to those who know the Lord. They form a parallel structure, with each (a) making a statement of the proper attitude toward God, followed by (b) a reason for trusting God. Break down these scriptures into the two components:

Verse 20

a._____

b._____

Verse 21

a._____

b._____

d. Epilogue: *Verse 22*

How does the psalmist conclude the psalm?

_____

_____

_____

_____

Turn *verses 20-22* into a personal prayer:

_____

_____

_____

_____

_____

_____

_____

_____

_____

_____

_____

Memorize

Psalm 33:20-21
Our soul waits for the LORD;
He is our help and our shield.
For our heart shall rejoice in Him,

Day Five – Descriptive Praise, Corporate

Israel used the Psalms in worship, as do many of the liturgical churches today. The most common ones were grouped as Royal or Enthronement Psalms, which were sung at the coronations of Judah's kings and, after the end of the monarchy, as they looked for the day when the Messiah would reign as King; Songs of Ascent, which were sung when the people climbed the mount to Jerusalem and as they entered the temple for holy days; and Hallel hymns. The Hallel hymns take two forms: Egyptian Hallel hymns, which look back to God's rescue of Israel from Egypt and are said as a unit on holy days (Psalms 113-118), and *pesukel dezimra* Hallel Psalms, which call God's people to praise Him for his character and are recited daily during Jewish morning services; they were initiated by Rabbi Jose in the second century and are recited during Jewish morning services (Psalms 145/6-150). Psalm 136 is called "the Great Hallel" in Jewish liturgy and is recited at the Passover meal.

<u>Read Psalm 136</u>

What is the refrain (repeated phrase)?

_____

In *verses 1-3*, what terms are used for God?

*Verse 1*_____

*Verse 2*_____

*Verse 3*_____

Verses 4-9 describe God's work in creation. What terms are used for His works?

*Verse 4*_____

*Verse 5*_____

*Verse 6*_____

*Verse 7*_____

*Verse 8*_____

*Verse 9*_____

Verses 10-22 describe God's deliverance of Israel from the Egyptians. List the different verbs that are used.

_____

_____

_____

_____

_____

_____

_____

What does this list say to *you* regarding God's power to deliver *you* as well?

_____

_____

_____

_____

_____

_____

_____

How would you use these verbs to describe God's work in *your* life leading to your salvation experience? Using the same words of the first lines of these verses, write a summary of how God worked to bring you out of your "Egypt" and into the "land" of freedom in Him.

_____

_____

_____

_____

_____

_____

_____

Verses 23-25
What does the psalmist say with regard to God's dealings with (a) His people and (b) all humanity?
a._____
b._____

Verse 26
What term is used for God in the epilogue?

_____

_____

How does this compare with the terms used in verses 1-3?

_____

_____

Write a prayer of praise using any combination of the verses you have studied this week. Bring it to the study to share with others.

_____
_____
_____
_____
_____
_____
_____
_____
_____
_____
_____

Memorize

Psalm 136:26
Oh, give thanks to the God of heaven!
For His mercy endures forever.

Week 6
Wisdom, Innocence, and Righteousness

This week, we embark on some rather complex concepts for some people: the quest for wisdom, the assertion of our innocence, and/or our righteousness in appealing to God to move on our behalf. The scriptures are clear about the value of gaining wisdom. Most people can see the value of seeking wisdom as described in the Proverbs and Psalms. However, when we come to the assertions of innocence and righteousness, especially with regard to asking God to act against our enemies, the concepts become more problematic. The purpose of this study is not to engage in some of the theological discussions that pertain to the matters of innocence and righteousness so much as to understand that the psalmists' use of these terms indicates that we, too, may appeal to God on these bases, as they constitute a part of His Word. We will look more closely at some of the considerations regarding innocence and righteousness in the next few days.

Day One – Value of Gaining Wisdom

The Proverbs, especially, are replete with verses concerning wisdom and its great benefit. We have a great promise, as well as an exhortation, in Proverbs 4:6-7, which states,

> Do not forsake [wisdom], and
> she will preserve you; Love her,
> and she will keep you.
> Wisdom is the principle thing;
> Therefore get wisdom.
> And in all your getting, get understanding.

<u>Read the Proverbs below</u> and note the main thought or teaching regarding the *value* of gaining wisdom:

*Proverbs 3:13-18*_____

*Proverbs 9:10*_____

*Proverbs 13:10*_____

What are some of the <u>advantages</u> of gaining wisdom?

*Proverbs 1:1-7*_____

*Proverbs 2:1-5*_____

*Proverbs 8:32-36*_____

*Proverbs 13:18*_____

*Proverbs 14:33*_____

*Proverbs 15:7*_____

*Proverbs 16:14*_____

*Proverbs 18:4*_____

*Proverbs 19:8*_____

*Proverbs 22:17, 18*_____

*Proverbs 24:3-5*_____

What <u>protection</u> does wisdom provide?

*Proverbs 5:1-6*_____

*Proverbs 7:4-5*_____

Summarize in your own words what you consider to be the most important points in these Proverbs.

_____

_____

_____

_____

_____

_____

_____

_____

_____

_____

Memorize Proverbs 4:6-7 (above)

Day Two – Prayer for Wisdom

<u>Read Psalm 1</u> again (we looked at it in Week One), this time in the context of wisdom.

Verse 1
How is the blessed person described in "negative" terms? (i.e., what does he/she *not* do?)

a._____

b._____

c._____

Put this description into *your* own words.

_____

_____

_____

_____

Verse 2
How is the blessed person described in "positive" terms? (i.e., what does he/she do?)

a._____

b._____

Verses 3-6

In the chart below fill in the differences in consequences for the blessed and the wicked (numbers represent verses):

Blessed	Wicked
3a	4b
3b	5
6a	6b

From your study yesterday in the Proverbs, what is it that demonstrates wisdom in this person's life?

_____

_____

To what extent is it part of *your* daily life?

_____

_____

<u>Read Psalm 37:30-34</u>

Verses 30-31
What characterizes a righteous person?

a._____

b._____

c._____

d._____

Verse 32
What characterizes the wicked?

a._____

b._____

We see in these verses the interrelationship between wisdom and those whom God deems "righteous." The "righteous" ones are known by their speech, as well as their actions. This is not to say, as some might argue, that we are *made* righteous by our speech and actions. Rather, we are *declared* righteous by faith in Jesus Christ, who "knew no sin but was made sin for us that we might be made the righteousness of God in Him" (II Corinthians 5:21). However, as James 2:20 notes, our faith is dead if it is not witnessed by our works; likewise, our righteousness should be evident in our speech.

Verse 33
What protection does the Lord provide the righteous (the one who speaks wisdom)?

a._____

b._____

Verse 34
What exhortation is given to the righteous?

_____

_____

What promise is given to the righteous?

_____

_____

In contrast to wisdom is foolishness, according to Scripture. We find that dire consequences come to those who refuse to gain wisdom.

Read Psalm 49:13-14

What does the psalmist say is their "shepherd"?

_____

What are the consequences of following that "shepherd"?

_____

How does this "shepherd" contrast with Jesus Christ, the Good Shepherd, and following Him (John 20:11, for example)?

_____

_____

_____

Read Psalm 111:10

What is the beginning of wisdom?

_____

In contrast, then, what would constitute foolishness?

_____

Using the Proverbs and Psalms above, write a prayer thanking God for His work in making you righteous before Him, for providing the means, through the Holy Spirit, for you to demonstrate your righteousness in what you say, and for the blessings that He promises to give the righteous.

_____

_____

_____

_____

_____

_____

_____

_____

_____

_____

_____

_____

Memorize

Psalm 111:10
The fear of the LORD is the beginning of wisdom;
A good understanding have all those who do His commandments;
His praise endures forever.

Day Three – Prayer of Innocence

In his commentary on the Psalms, Dietrich Bonhoeffer made some interesting observations concerning the prayers of innocence, noting that some evangelical Christians find it offensive that the innocence of devout individuals is as prominent as is their guilt. However, as Bonhoeffer pointed out, "It is characteristic of the prayer of the Christian to hold fast to this innocence and justification which has come to him, appealing to God's word and thanking for it. So not only are we permitted, but directly obligated—provided we take God's action to us at all seriously—to pray in all humiliation and certainty: 'I was blameless before him and I kept myself from guilt.'"

Another point to keep in mind is that the psalmist is not declaring his lack of sin but his innocence with regard to the situation or the charges that have been leveled against him. Hence, the Psalms of Innocence provide good patterns for praying when we have been unjustly accused of something or treated unjustly. Today, we are going to look at portions of Psalm 25. Other Psalms you might like to review are Psalms 17 and 26:6-12.

Read Psalm 25:1-3, 16-21

In these two passages, David calls out to God to deliver him from his enemies, claiming his own innocence in the situation.

Verses 1-3
How does David express his confidence in God *(vss. 1, 2a)*?

What is his concern (*vs. 2b*)?

_____

What does he say about God's faithfulness (*vs. 3*)?

_____

_____

Enemies are not necessarily people, as was the case with David. They may be spiritual beings that seek to destroy or devour us (I Peter 5:8-9). Indeed, even those individuals who seek to do us harm are actually energized by the spiritual world. Hence, David's cry can apply to all of us. The question is: How do we respond when someone seeks to do us harm? How do *you* respond?

_____

_____

_____

_____

_____

_____

Verses 16-21
In this portion of the Psalm, David expresses his innermost emotional pain to God, he articulates the problem he faces, and he cries for help.

Verses 16-17a
What words does David use to describe his feelings?

_____

_____

_____

Have *you* ever felt like this?

_____

If so, when? How did you handle the situation?

_____

_____

_____

_____

_____

Verses 17b-18
Where or to whom does David turn? What does he request?
a._____

b._____

c._____

Verse 19
How does David describe the situation?

_____

_____

Verses 20-21
What is David's main concern (his physical or spiritual safety)?

_____

_____

What words does he use to express his innocence in the matter?

_____

_____

What principles do you derive from David's expressions in the Psalm that you could apply to *your* life in the midst of being attacked?

_____

_____

_____

_____

_____

_____

_____

_____

Memorize

Psalm 25:12-13
Who is the man that fears the LORD?
He shall teach him in the way He chooses.
He himself shall dwell in prosperity,
And his descendants shall inherit the earth.

Day Four – Prayer of Righteousness

Much like an expression of innocence, the expression of righteousness must be viewed in the context in which it is made. The Hebrew term for righteousness (צדקה) and the nouns and verbs derived from it have a wide range of meaning. In the context of the Psalms we shall look at today, it means to stand firm before God in the midst of trials or, as is the case with innocence, when falsely accused and the object of slander. Another concept is that of maintaining integrity in the midst of a corrupt society. Then, of course, we have the Psalms that we can pray today as believers who stand in Christ's righteousness, purchased for us on the Cross of Calvary. Psalm 32:1-2 is one such expression:

How blessed is he whose transgression is forgiven,
Whose sin is covered!
How blessed is the man to whom the Lord does not impute iniquity,
And in whose spirit there is no deceit.

Today, we are going to concentrate on Psalm 26.

<u>Read Psalm 26 *several* times.</u>

Verse 1
What can we presume to be David's situation? What word provides that clue?

_____

Verse 2
What does David ask the Lord to do about his spiritual condition?
a._____
b._____

Verse 3a
David can confidently ask this examination of the Lord because of his confidence in what?

_____

Verses 3b-5
What negative things does David mention, as in those things he does *not* do?
a._____
b._____
c._____
d._____

What distinction do you think David is making between himself and the world or his enemies?

_____

How does *your* life differ from your neighbor's or the world's?

_____
_____
_____
_____
_____

Ask the Holy Spirit to reveal those things that you need to turn from or remove from your life. What changes do *you* need to make?

_____

_____

_____

_____

Verses 6-7
David declares his intentions to worship and to "wash his hands in innocence." Spurgeon points out that this is a public action separating the individual from all association with a deed and any accompanying accusations (much as Pilate "washed his hands" of the affair with regard to Jesus). In the Levitical system of sacrifices, the priests washed their hands before offering sacrifices. In the context of going to the altar, David alludes to the Levitical system and declares his determination to cleanse himself of all iniquity before approaching God. What is his intent upon approaching the altar (Verse 7)?

_____

_____

_____

_____

_____

_____

Verse 8
How does David express his feelings regarding "God's house"?

_____

_____

What is *your* attitude about going to church?

_____

_____

_____

_____

Verses 9-10
David calls upon God to deliver him. What is his main concern?

_____

_____

What assurance do we have that we shall not have our "souls taken away along with sinners"?

_____

_____

Verses 11-12
These verses represent another shift – from the description of the wicked to David's confidence in his own integrity. How does he express his confidence and his relationship with the Lord?

_____

_____

_____

What does "even place" mean to you? How would this concept apply to *your* life?

_____

_____

_____

_____

_____

Memorize

Psalm 26:11-12
But as for me, I will walk in my integrity;
Redeem me, and be merciful to me.
My foot stands in an even place;
In the congregation I will bless the LORD.

Day Five – Imprecatory Prayers

Today, we come to what is universally considered the most difficult type of Psalm to understand: the "imprecatory" Psalm. Hassell Bullock, a noted Old Testament scholar, has pointed out some of the problems associated with understanding these psalms and their use, as well as a common thread, at least in three of them (35, 69, 109). He says that "personal vindictiveness is placed in a larger context. The psalmist consigned the matter to God. There was absolutely no effort on his part to take personal revenge. He seemed to have been aware of the Mosaic principle, 'Vengeance is Mine' (Deut. 32:35)." Bob Deffinbaugh notes that the bases for praying in this respect are (1) David's claim of his own innocence in the matter and (2) the iniquity of his enemies, who are opposed to God. In this regard, we can see that the imprecatory psalms can be used to pray against the spiritual forces that are behind the actions of those who attack us, for as Paul reminds us: "our struggle is not against flesh and blood, but against the rulers, against the authorities, against the powers of this dark world and against the spiritual forces of evil in the heavenly realms" (Ephesians 6:12). In addition, we have the confidence of knowing that these Psalms are God's Word and, if we pray them in dependence upon Him, He receives them and acts upon them in accordance with His will.

Read Psalm 109

This prayer of David's has the two points noted above: his innocence and the enemies' iniquity.

Verse 1
How does David address God?

_____

What does this say to you about David's relationship with the Lord?

_____

Review the lessons we did last week on praise and write down some of the terms David uses:

_____

_____

What request does he make of God?

_____

Verse 2
How does David describe the attack he is experiencing?

_____

_____

_____

_____

What words does he use to maintain his innocence?

_____

How does his behavior differ from theirs?

_____

_____

_____

Verses 6-15
These are the types of verses that people find difficult to accept because they appear to be very vindictive. One consideration is that these people are covenant offenders and they have brought these very conditions upon the faithful, so David is acting with the concept of "an eye for an eye." David's requests or curses can be divided into several categories; put them in your own words:

*Verse 8*_____

*Verses 9-10*_____

*Verses 11-12*_____

*Verse 13*_____

*Verse 14-15*_____

*Verses 16-21*_____

What reason does David give for making these requests?

*Verse 16a*_____

*Verse 16b*_____

*Verse 17a*_____

*Verse 17b*_____

*Verse 18a*_____

What does David seek in return?

*Verse 17b*_____

*Verse 18b*_____

*Verses 19-20*_____

*Verse 21*_____

At this point in the psalm, a "shift" occurs: David turns his prayer toward his own situation and needs. In the shift in verse 21, how does David address God?

_____

On what basis does he make his appeal?

_____

_____

_____

Verses 22-25
How does David describe his condition? This description gives us an insight into the depths of his anguish.

_____

_____

_____

_____

_____

Have *you* ever felt this desperate? How did you handle your situation?

_____

_____

_____

_____

_____

Verses 26-29
David once again cries out and asks for God's help. What is the basis of his appeal?

_____

_____

What extended purpose does David desire?

_____

_____

_____

In the New Testament, our Lord Jesus Christ gives us new instructions.

Read Matthew 5:43-48 and Luke 6:27-28

What is to be our response to:

our enemies? _____

those who persecute us? _____

those who hate us? _____

those who curse us? _____

those who abuse us? _____

Keep in mind that Jesus' instructions do not preclude the need on occasion to separate ourselves from abusive people and enemies, especially when children and other vulnerable individuals are involved. That matter is a separate issue. What we are seeing here is the means for us to have inner healing, to initiate in prayer an attitude and a response different from those of the world, and to glorify God.

Verses 30-31 (Psalm 109)
David returns to his initial praise – it is a "circular" element of the poem. Put David's remarks into your own words:

_____

_____

_____

_____

_____

_____

_____

Memorize

Luke 6:22

Blessed are you when men hate you,
and when they exclude you,
And revile you, and cast out your name as evil,
For the Son of Man's sake.
Rejoice in that day and leap for joy!
For indeed your reward is great in heaven,
For in like manner their fathers did to the prophets.

Conclusion

This completes our introduction to using the Psalms as a basis for prayer. This study is intended, as noted above, to lay a foundation for you to build upon. May you be blessed in your study and may you grow mightily in the Lord as you apply His Word to the everyday events of life.

The LORD bless you and keep you;
The LORD make His face shine upon you,
And be gracious to you;
The LORD lift up His countenance upon you,
and give you peace.

Numbers 6:24

References

Bonhoeffer, Dietrich. *Psalms: The Prayer Book of the Bible*. Minneapolis, MN: Augsburg Publishing House, 1970, 1974

Bullock, C. Hassell. *An Introduction to the Old Testament Poetic Books*. Chicago, IL: Moody Press, 1979, 1988

Calvin, Psalm 26.
http://www.sacredtexts.com/chr/calvin/cc08/cc08031.htm

Coffman, James Burton. "Commentary on Psalm 26" in *Coffman Commentaries on the Old and New Testament.*
http://www.studylight.org/com/bcc/view.cgi?book=ps&chapter=026

Deffinbaugh, Bob. *A Psalm for All Seasons: Studies in the Book of Psalms.*
http://bible.org/series/psalm-all-seasons-studies-book-psalms

Estes, Daniel J. *Handbook on the Wisdom Books and Psalms*. Grand Rapids, MI: Baker Academic, 2005

LaRondelle, Hans K. "Sermons from Psalms.*" Ministry: International Journal for Pastors.*
https://www.ministrymagazine.org/archive/1984/May/sermons-from-psalms

Penn, William. *Some Fruits of Solitude/More Fruits of Solitude.*
http://www.bartleby.com/1/3/

Ross, Allen P. *A Commentary on the Psalms*, Vol. 1. Grand Rapids, MI: Kregel Publications, 2011

Schmutzer, Andrew J. and David M. Howard, Jr (eds). *The Psalms: Language for All Seasons of the Soul.* Chicago, IL: Moody Press, 2013

Wright, N.T. *The Case for the Psalms: Why They Are Essential.* New York, NY: HarperColllins Publishers, 2013

Memory Scriptures

"This Book of the Law shall not depart from your mouth;
but you shall meditate on it day and night,
so that you may be careful to do according to all that is written in it.
For then you will make your way prosperous and then you will have good success."
(Joshua 1:8)

Happy is the man who finds wisdom, And the man who gains understanding;
For her proceeds are better than the profits of silver And her gain than fine gold.
She is more precious than rubies,
And all the things you may desire cannot compare with her.
(Proverbs 3:13-15)

Week 1

<u>Psalm 119:97</u>

Oh, how I love Your law!
It is my meditation all the day.

<u>Psalm 1:1-2</u>

Blessed is the man
Who walks not in the counsel of the ungodly,
Nor stands in the path of sinners,
Nor sits in the seat of the scornful;
But his delight is in the law of the Lord,
And in His law he meditates day and night.

<u>Psalm 1:3</u>

He shall be like a tree
Planted by the rivers of water,
That brings forth its fruit in its season,
Whose leaf also shall not whither;
And whatever he does shall prosper.

<u>Psalm 1:4</u>

The ungodly are not so,
But are like chaff which the wind drives away.

Psalm 1:5-6

Therefore the ungodly shall not stand in the judgment,
Nor sinners in the congregation of the righteous;
For the Lord knows the way of the righteous,
But the way of the ungodly shall perish.

Week 2

Proverbs 3:5,6

Trust in the Lord with all your heart,
And lean not on your own understanding;
In all your ways acknowledge Him,
And He shall direct your paths.

Psalm 59:17

To you, O my Strength,
I will sing praises;
For God is my defense
My God of mercy.

Psalm 42:11

Why are you cast down, O my soul
And why are you disquieted within me?
Hope in God;
For I shall again praise Him,
The help of my countenance and my God.

Psalm 25:4-5

Show me Your ways, O Lord;
Teach me your paths.
Lead me in Your truth and teach me,
For you are the God of my salvation;
On You I wait all the day.

Psalm 30:5b

Weeping may endure for a night,
But joy comes in the morning.

Week 3

II Chronicles 16:9

For the eyes of the Lord run to and fro
throughout the whole earth,
to show Himself strong on behalf of those
whose heart is loyal to Him.

Psalm 107:1,2

Oh give thanks to the Lord, for He is good,
For his mercy endures forever.
Let the redeemed of the Lord say so
Whom He has redeemed from the hand of the enemy

I Chronicles 7:14

If My people, who are called by My name
will humble themselves, and pray
and seek My face,
and turn from their wicked ways,
then I will hear from heaven,
and will forgive their sin, and heal their land.

Proverbs 30:5

Every word of is pure;
He is a shield to those who put their trust in Him.

Psalm 6:8-10

Depart from me, all you workers of iniquity;

For the Lord has heard the voice of my weeping.

The Lord has heard my supplication;
The Lord receives my prayer.
Let all my enemies be ashamed and greatly troubled;
Let them turn back and be ashamed suddenly.

Week 4

Psalm 53:2-3

God looks down from heaven upon the children of men To see if
there are any who understand, who seek God.
Every one of them has turn aside;
They have together become corrupt;
There is none who does good, No, not one.

Psalm 51:17

The sacrifices of God are a broken spirit,
A broken and a contrite heart —
These, O God, You will not despise.

Psalm 32:1, 2

Blessed is he whose transgression is forgiven,
Whose sin is covered.
Blessed is the man to whom the Lord does not impute iniquity,
And in whose spirit there is no deceit.

Psalm 12:1,2

I beseech you therefore, brethren, by the mercies of God,
that you present your bodies a living sacrifice,
holy, acceptable to God, which is your reasonable service.
And do not be conformed to this world,
but be transformed by the renewing of your mind,
that you may prove what is that good and
acceptable and perfect will of God.

I John 1:9

If we confess our sins,
He is faithful and just to forgive our sins
and to cleanse us of all unrighteousness.

Week 5

Proverbs 9:10

The fear of the Lord is the beginning of wisdom,
And the knowledge of the Holy One
is understanding.

Psalm 34:8,9

Oh, taste and see that the Lord is good;
Blessed is the man who trusts in Him!
Oh, fear the LORD, you His saints!
There is no want to those who fear Him.

Psalm 104:33-34

I will sing to the LORD as long as I live;
I will sing praise to my God while I have my being.
May my meditation be sweet to Him;
I will be glad in the LORD.

Psalm 33:20-22

Our soul waits for the LORD;
He is our help and our shield.
For our heart shall rejoice in Him,
Because we have trusted in His holy name.

Psalm 136:26

Oh, give thanks to the God of heaven!
For His mercy endures forever.

Week 6

Proverbs 4:6,7

Do not forsake [wisdom], and she will preserve you;
Love her, and she will keep you.
Wisdom is the principle thing; Therefore get wisdom.
And in all your getting, get understanding

Psalm 111:10

The fear of the LORD is the beginning of wisdom;
A good understanding have all those who do His
commandments;
His praise endures forever.

Psalm 25:12-13

Who is the man that fears the LORD?
He shall teach him in the way He chooses.
He himself shall dwell in prosperity,
And his descendants shall inherit the earth.

Psalm 26:11-12

But as for me, I will walk in my integrity;
Redeem me, and be merciful to me.
My foot stands in an even place;
In the congregation I will bless the LORD.

Luke 6:22

Blessed are you when men hate you,
and when they exclude you,
And revile you, and cast out your name as evil,
For the Son of Man's sake.
Rejoice in that day and leap for joy!
For indeed your reward is great in heaven,
For in like manner their fathers did to the prophets.

Psalms Used in This Study

Week 1
Psalm 119
Psalm 77
Psalm 1

Week 2
Psalm 73
Psalm 37
Psalm 52
Psalm 64
Psalm 56
Psalm 59
Psalm 58
Psalm 13
Psalm 42
Psalm 22
Psalm 25
Psalm 38
Psalm 88
Psalm 89
Psalm 71
Psalm 116
Psalm 34
Psalm 46
Psalm 30

Week 3
Psalm 67
Psalm 91
Psalm 107
Psalm 72
Psalm 18
Psalm 23
Psalm 88
Psalm 121
Psalm 142
Psalm 7
Psalm 55
Psalm 61
Psalm 64
Psalm 23
Psalm 37
Psalm 22
Psalm 42
Psalm 65
Psalm 31
Psalm 70
Psalm 71
Psalm 6

Week 4
Psalm 51
Psalm 53
Psalm 32
Psalm 85
Psalm 32
Psalm 51
Psalm 86
Psalm 130

Week 5
Psalm 34
Psalm 104
Psalm 33
Psalm 136

Week 6
Psalm 1
Psalm 37
Psalm 49
Psalm 111
Psalm 25
Psalm 26
Psalm 109

Proverbs Used in This Study

Proverbs 1

Proverbs 2

Proverbs 3

Proverbs 4

Proverbs 6

Proverbs 8

Proverbs 9

Proverbs 10

Proverbs 11

Proverbs 12

Proverbs 13

Proverbs 14

Proverbs 15

Proverbs 16

Proverbs 17

Proverbs 18

Proverbs 19

Proverbs 22

Proverbs 24

Proverbs 30

Personal Notes

www.ingramcontent.com/pod-product-compliance
Lightning Source LLC
LaVergne TN
LVHW051352080426
835509LV00020BB/3403